To Cynthia,
May you glimpse the glory of God at every step of your new adventure.
Much love, Ros

Index

The Laughing Rabbi

Nothing ever happens here. The last time anything noteworthy occurred was when Benjamin's bullock unexpectedly dropped dead on its way to the winepress, overturning the bullock-cart and sending ripe red bunches of grapes tumbling down the hill to land in a sticky puddle of juice at the bottom.

So the news that was buzzing round the village had caused a stir, and even I was alive with curiosity. Of course, the stories were exaggerated, of that I had no doubt. Whenever a gifted young rabbi attracted an enthusiastic following, the tales of his doings were embellished with every telling. Nevertheless, even my sceptical old heart thrilled with pleasurable expectancy at the rumour that he was coming to our synagogue the next day.

The anticipation wasn't likely to keep me awake. When every step is an effort and every movement pain, exhaustion engulfs you as soon as you lie down.

So when supper was ended and the light beginning to fade, I shuffled over to my straw-filled palliasse and placed a hand on the rickety stool which my daughter-in-law had carefully placed beside it, on which to steady myself. As gently as I could, I lowered myself to my knees, then leant forward until my head touched the linen of the palliasse, and then rolled over onto my side. It had taken me a while to perfect this technique, but it meant I could go to bed unassisted. Once on my side, I reached out for the cloak which lay rolled up on the floor, and pulled it over me as protection from the night chill.

When I awoke the next morning with the first rays of sun slicing through the dancing specks of dust from the little hole at the top of the wall, I felt as excited as a child, and it took me some moments to recall why. The young rabbi from Galilee was visiting our synagogue today, and we would see for ourselves how much truth there was in the gossip about him.

Nobody expected me to go to synagogue any more, not on the Sabbath, not even on feast days. Since the arrival of my grandson, my daughter-in-law was too busy to help me out of bed in the mornings, and without her assistance it took so long that the service was over before I was ready. But today I was determined to be there, so I started early.

First I rolled up the cloak and tried to toss it over the stool, where I would be able to reach it without bending down. It took many attempts, but finally the top of the cloak hooked over the top of the stool and stayed there.

With difficulty, I pushed myself up into a sideways sitting position, and from there, managed to get onto my knees. Reaching up beyond where I could tilt my head to look, I grasped the stool with both arms and, unable to suppress a cry of pain, I clawed my way to my feet until I stood, breathless, staring at the floor, which was my only view of the world since the disease had eaten away at my back and I had become more and more bent over. In fact, it had been eighteen long years since I last stood erect and looked anybody in the eye. Taking the cloak in my hand, I eased myself onto the stool and after many attempts, succeeded in pulling the cloak around my shoulders, far harder than it sounds since my hands could no longer reach to the back of my neck.

My feet were already sandalled. I had given up removing my sandals at night; the effort of putting them back on in the morning was just too great. When my husband was still alive, he had found a sturdy branch with a forked top which he had whittled down into a comfortable handle, so that I could have a walking staff to support me. Taking the branch which was leaning against the wall, I made my way to the centre of our home, where my daughter-in-law had just placed warm bread and a fresh jug of foaming milk on the table.

"Well mother," smiled Elias, "this is early for you!"

I gave him a quiet nod. I had told no one of my intention to attend synagogue today. "I'm coming with you to hear the young rabbi," I announced.

We left the home together, Miriam following Elias, the baby held against her breast by a shawl tied around her shoulders. This I could not see, but I knew because it was how I had carried Elias twenty-five years earlier.

As usual I stared at the dirt track beneath my feet, enjoying the places where the pasture encroached on the roadside, and the grass running along for a few yards made a pleasant change of scene.

Every time I walked this road I stopped outside our neighbours' farm. Their fields sloped away downhill and their olive trees, devoid of any shelter from the prevailing winds, bent so low over the road across the boundary of their land that even I could see some of the glossy dark leaves and fat olives. I always took a moment to relish the sight.

Today I seemed to notice these things even more – as if I was really present to the present moment, instead of being always on my way to somewhere else or distracted by the pain.

I took my place, resting on my stick, at the back of the synagogue where the other women stood. I couldn't look up to see the young man's face but I saw the hem of his tunic and the worn-out sandals as he walked past to take his place on the bimah.

We sang a hymn and then the synagogue ruler must have handed him the scroll; I heard it being unrolled. With a voice of musical clarity he began to read the words of the law: "If there is a poor man with you, one of your brothers, in any of your towns, you shall not harden your heart nor close your hand from your poor brother, but you shall generously open your hand and lend him whatever he needs."

Then I heard him rolling up the scroll and he began to teach, words which were like balm to every aching soul in the room.

"Blessed are you poor, for yours is the kingdom of heaven. Blessed are you who mourn, for you shall be comforted. Blessed are you meek, for you shall inherit the earth." When he finished speaking there was an awed silence, for none of us had heard any teaching like it before. But nobody expected what happened next.

I heard him step down from the bimah, and his sandalled feet scuffed across the stone floor of the synagogue. I saw them approaching again, fringed by the bottom of his tunic. I waited for him to pass on by, but he didn't.

He stopped right in front of me, and then, bending his knees, he crouched down until his face was level with mine. And what a face it was – alight with laughter, as though he knew a hilarious secret that the rest of us were not privy to. His penetrating eyes looked deep into mine, and I darted my gaze to the floor. Women didn't look men in the eye, especially rabbis, and yet he seemed to be inviting me to.

What could he possibly want with me? I thought of the stories I had heard, heard and dismissed as exaggerated.

"Look at me." There was authority in the voice and I did not resist. As I raised my gaze to meet his, the hilarity lit up his face again and he said, pronouncing each word with great deliberateness, "Woman, you are freed from your sickness."

Before I had time to respond, he placed his hands on me and I felt all the pain seep out of my body, as though a drain hole had been opened in the soles of my feet. And then I felt a surge of warmth which began at the base of my back and flowed up into my shoulders. The next thing I knew I was standing erect, free from pain, and looking the world in the eye. He grasped my hands, laughing out loud with delight, and swung me around and around.

A burst of praise erupted from deep within me. I had to glorify God for what He had done, and I broke into the words of a Psalm that I had learned as a small girl: "Bless the Lord, O my soul, and all that is within me bless His holy name. Bless the Lord, O my soul, and forget not all His benefits. He forgives all my sins; He heals all my diseases; He redeems my life from the pit."

Another voice joined in with mine. The young rabbi continued the praise in unison with me: "He crowns my life with lovingkindness and tender mercies; He satisfies my years with good things so that my youth is renewed like the eagle's." And so it was.

As I turned and left, clutching to my heart the gift I had received, I became aware of a commotion behind me, men's agitated voices. I caught the words "healing, "Sabbath", "woman" and "improper". I stopped and looked back at the young rabbi surrounded by angry men. He saw me look, and shook his head at me, as if to say, "This is my problem. You leave it; I'll deal with it."

I fairly skipped back up the road to home and, throwing my cloak onto my bed, rolled up the sleeves of my tunic and began preparing the midday meal while my daughter-in-law fed the baby. As I worked I kept recalling the light of laughter in that young man's eyes and an answering chuckle bubbled up from somewhere deep within me. I sang as I worked, certain beyond doubt that more than just my body had been healed that day. Luke 13.10 – 13

Waiter, there's a mouse in my soup!

My father had an interesting job. He worked, at various times, for several different missionary societies. His job involved paying pastoral visits to missionaries and took him to countries as diverse as India and Bolivia, Afghanistan and Liberia among many others. As a result he had many stories to tell of the adventures he encountered on his way.

I remember in particular his account of a visit to two missionary ladies in Senegal. They lived, like the people among whom they worked, in a simple mud hut with a straw roof. These ladies had prepared some soup for his visit, and when dinner time came one of them set the bowl of soup down in front of him.

Just at that precise moment, a mouse in the thatch above them gave birth, and the unfortunate offspring landed in my father's bowl of soup. Without turning a hair, one of the ladies whisked his bowl away from under his nose and dealt with the baby mouse. She brought the bowl of soup back and they continued with their meal.

My father (who always made a point of gratefully eating whatever was set in front of him) said afterwards that he didn't ask whether it was the same bowl of soup with the mouse simply removed, or whether it was a fresh serving. Being hungry, he tucked in and was thankful.

So here I am, facing the next chapter of my life. The tears come less frequently and the future looks appetising. So am I going to sit and complain about what fell into my bowl, or am I going to attack what's left in it with relish?

St Paul said, "For I am convinced that neither death nor life, neither angels nor demons, neither the present nor the future, nor any powers, neither height nor depth, nor anything else in all creation, will be able to separate us from the love of God that is in Christ Jesus our Lord." In other words, whatever the future holds, it will all be permeated with the love of God manifested in the presence of Jesus. What's not to like?

I recently applied (successfully, praise God!) for the job of Training Resources Developer with Through the Roof, a charity whose mission is to change lives through disabled people; a mission it accomplishes by providing life-changing opportunities for disabled people, and equipping churches to do the same. As part of the interview process I had to prepare a presentation which included a Biblical theology of disability.

I have been teaching disability awareness in schools and colleges for many years, but I had never before sat down and thought through the Biblical basis for what I was so passionate about. Here are some of my thoughts – not all of which could be included in my presentation because of time, but all of which I wrote down and thought through as part of my preparation.

When we look at the Biblical basis for anything, our first starting point has to be Jesus. He was the most inclusive person ever to walk this earth. He embraced the other gender (women, obviously!), people of other ethnicities (such as the Syro-Phoenician woman whose daughter he healed), other faiths (such as the centurion who undoubtedly worshipped Roman gods) and those of other social classes (such as tax collectors and prostitutes). Some have even argued that, in Roman culture, it's highly likely that the servant healed by Jesus was also the centurion's gay partner. Certainly Jesus had no hesitation in welcoming unreservedly people whose behaviour he could not and did not sanction, such as the woman taken in adultery, or the young ruler whose greed held him captive to his money.

In particular, Jesus always saw beyond the disability to the whole person. That's why he did not allow the woman who touched the hem of his garment to slink away anonymously but called her forward publicly, honoured her faith, and ensured that she was not simply physically healed, but made whole. Whereas the church has at times seen disabled people as a collection of body parts – blind eyes in need of sight, perhaps, or cerebral palsied legs in need of healing and strength. I am personally convinced that healing is a part of what Jesus' atonement won for us, and I am committed to praying for people to be healed, and expecting to see God's power at work in them. I am also convinced of God's sovereignty and that He doesn't have to deal with everyone I encounter in the way that I tell Him to!

The trouble is that often, in our eagerness to see disabled people healed we, the non-disabled members of Christ's church, have overlooked their current worth and potential, and have given them the message "you're not acceptable the way you are" – and I'm certain that Jesus never made anybody feel that way. On the contrary, in one of His parables, Jesus mentioned disabled people as those who should be given pride of place at the feast table in His kingdom. As we read the Gospel accounts of his encounters with disabled people, it's easy to picture the delight on His face as He set them free not just from their physical limitations, but from the limiting self-image their disability had imposed on them, and showed them the glory of their true self as God had first created them to be.

There are some Old Testament stories, too, that should inform our attitudes towards disabled members of our communities. When David became king of Israel, he looked for someone of the house of Saul to whom he could show kindness for his friend Jonathan's sake. The only surviving member of Saul's family was Mephibosheth. At the time of the overthrow of Saul's house, his nurse had picked him up to run to safety but had fallen with him in her arms, leaving him with a permanent disability. David welcomed him as part of his household, and for the rest of his life he ate at the king's own table. It struck me as I read this passage in 2 Samuel 9 firstly, that David did not pity Mephibosheth because of his disability. It was who he was – Jonathan's son – that dictated David's response to him. His disability was irrelevant. Secondly, when David discovered that Saul's only living relative was a disabled man, that didn't alter his intent towards him. He honoured him exactly as he would have done if he had been a strong warrior. And finally, the whole story provides a wonderful metaphor for the church, with disabled and non-disabled people seated side by side, with equal honour, at the table in God's kingdom.

I also looked at the story in 2 Kings 7 of four men with a contagious skin disease who were living as outcasts from the community of Israel. At a time when their own people were reduced to such a level of starvation that they had actually resorted, in their desperation, to cannibalism, these four men discovered the enemy camp deserted and full of food and other spoils and provisions. Rather than keep this good fortune to themselves, they said, "We are not doing right. This day is a day of good news, but we are keeping silent; if we wait until morning light, punishment will overtake us. Now therefore come, let us go and tell the king's household." So they went and shared their good news with the rest of their community. This strikes me as a very powerful metaphor for the church, with disabled people not seen as outcasts or victims to be pitied, but as active contributors to the life and health of God's people.

I also thought about St Paul's vision for the church. In Colossians 1.28 he sets out his mission statement, "To present everyone complete in Christ." Every time someone new comes through the doors of our church or expresses a desire to add themselves to us, we should be asking, "What does this person need, to become complete in Christ?" It would be silly to ask what do disabled people need to become complete in Christ – a bit like asking what do the blue-eyed, or the left-handed, need to become complete in Christ? The answer is that we are all individuals, each with our own relationship with God. As with anyone else in the church, a disabled church member needs people to get to know them, to learn what their gifting is, where they can serve and build up the church, and what their weaker areas are, where they could use support and encouragement from the rest of the body of Christ.

Legend has it that in Mediaeval France the Catholic Church taught that people with learning disabilities were placed by God in communities in order that people should be able to reverence and honour them as they would reverence and honour Christ Himself. These people became known as "Chréstiens", Little Christs. This word – at first with no derogatory connotation – came into the English language as the word cretin, which sadly, like so many other terms surrounding disability, became devalued, and degenerated into an offensive insult.

It is very important that as we seek to allow disabled people to play their full part in the life of the church, we make sure to use inclusive language. When I was the Disability Advisor at a College of Further Education, I attempted to ban the use of the term "special needs" because it seemed to me to be just another way of isolating disabled students and making them feel different from everybody else, and because I had heard children in the playground at my daughter's school hurling it as a term of abuse at one another. The origin of the term "handicapped" is in dispute, but one possibility is that it dates back to the days when it was thought that disabled people were fit only to beg for a living, and would sit patiently hoping that you would place your hand in their cap with a donation for them. For this reason, handicapped is felt quite keenly by many disabled people as a demeaning term, and I would like to see it eliminated from our vocabulary as Christians. If this seems like "political correctness gone mad" it's worth considering the words of Jesus, that "out of the overflow of the heart the mouth speaks". It's the language we use casually and unthinkingly that reveals the attitudes we really harbour in our hearts towards one another.

In preparing my presentation, I reflected on a book I read many years ago, the autobiography of Rev Alyn Haskey who I was privileged to meet a few times before his sad death last year. In his book he described an incident when he was training for ordination. All the students were in the dining hall when the fire alarm sounded. They all jumped up and evacuated the building leaving Alyn, who could not propel his own wheelchair, sitting at the table. A few minutes later one of his fellow students came running back in very upset and said, "I'm so sorry Alyn, I forgot you were in a wheelchair!" Alyn observed that it was one of the best moments of his life, because people had stopped seeing his wheelchair and were seeing him for the person that he really was.

So for me it's going to be a real privilege to serve the body of Christ in my new role by helping churches to see the wealth of gift and beauty that God has placed among them in the form of many disabled people.

Fearfully and Wonderfully Made

A teacher friend has asked me to go and talk to his year 11 class about why I don't see disability as valid grounds for abortion. I hope my lesson will dispel some myths about life with a disability. I will tell them that I did not know that my daughter would be disabled (she wasn't born with her disability, but became disabled at about 9 weeks old) but that even if I could have known in advance about her limitations, I would not have opted for an abortion, and that all my experience in the 30 years since confirms that opinion.

There are three main arguments which are usually put forward in support of abortion on the grounds of disability. These are firstly that it's not fair on the parents to have such a burden placed on them, one which will disrupt their lives for the rest of their lives, secondly that it's not fair on the siblings to have a brother or sister who takes the lion's share of the attention, and thirdly that it's not fair to bring a child into the world who is going to experience suffering, and be unable to attain the accomplishments their peers achieve. I will take these three arguments and try to give them a different perspective, one which the media seldom presents.

Has raising a disabled child been burdensome to our family? Has it had a great impact on our lives? Well of course it changed many things. Meals become difficult when a child has severe physical difficulties in swallowing food. Family relationships become strained when one person has difficulty in communicating with the other family members. Excursions become complicated once a wheelchair always has to be taken into account. You can't wake up one sunny morning in the school holidays and decide to jump on a train for a family outing, because rail travel with a wheelchair is supposed to be booked forty-eight hours in advance. As Dan Batten once wrote in Disability Now, "Woe betide the disabled person who decides on a whim to go out for the day." Exhaustion is a permanent companion when a child who can't turn over in bed needs attention eight or ten times a night. All these things I will be realistic about.

But the big question is, has this ruined our lives? There's no doubt that a child's disability dominates family life. You look back over the decades and see a very different journey from the one you thought you were going to travel when you set out. But so what? All kinds of things make your life different from the one you had planned. Sickness, accident and bereavement can strike at any time. Statistically, in a class of thirty children, between three and four will end up as carers of disabled people, either their own children or older relatives. Some will already be young carers.

When my daughter was born, despite already having a two year old, I was a very self-centred twenty-five year old. My observation throughout life tells me that selfish people are generally more unhappy than unselfish ones. Having to put someone else's needs always before my own has made me a very different person, but crucially it has made me a much happier one. When life is tough you learn to notice and appreciate the small joys you might otherwise overlook. I am amazed at how resourceful that rather helpless twenty-five year old has become. I no longer sweat the small stuff! Has having a disabled child ruined my life? No, it has made it harder and far, far richer.

How about the siblings? Their life is going to be disrupted if a brother or sister with high dependency needs comes into the family. There's no way to avoid this, although a wise parent will grab with both hands every offer of help with the disabled child in order to maximize opportunity for one-to-one time with their other children. My daughter Ellen is the middle one of three. It's true that when she was growing up relations with her older sister were strained for a time, and the disrupted nights took their toll. Her other sister is younger by nine years, and was not yet three when Ellen went to boarding school during the week, coming home only at weekends and school holidays. That made the strain on her less than on her older sister. Nevertheless, the three of them have grown up very close and affectionate, and although they will agree that their lives were perhaps harder than those of their peers, they too will agree that their lives were also richer. They learned patience, unselfishness, and how to find those diamonds of joy in days of hardship, qualities that will stand them in good stead for the rest of their lives.

Interestingly, I note that among my friends who have disabled children, many if not most of the siblings have ended up working in the caring professions – doctors, nurses, social workers, speech and language therapists, children's charity workers and church ministers. Far from turning their backs on people with disabilities or other difficulties in life, their experiences have made them want to spend their lives among such people. So their childhood can't have been all bad.

The issue of the disabled child's suffering is a serious one, and something that can't be made light of. The question is, how many people's suffering is so bad that it would have been better if they had never been born? Disability is a vast spectrum, and when I ask those school students who favour abortion for disability, "Where would you draw the line?" the most common answers are that if the child will have a serious learning disability or be unable to walk, abortion would be acceptable. Ellen fits both these criteria. Although she has a few pockets of real intelligence, and reasonably good ability to communicate, she experiences the frustrations of severe autism, and has never been able to walk or even stand or sit unsupported.

Undoubtedly she has experienced more suffering in her life than her sisters. She had her first major orthopaedic operation at about twenty months old, and although I am starting to lose count, I believe she's had over thirty operations since. I have always stayed with her while she is anaesthetised (apart from one life-threatening operation where I couldn't bring myself to do it and my husband stood in for me) and even now after all these years I still go and cry in the chapel once she disappears into the operating theatre and the doors close behind her. And when life becomes too unbearable, she often resorts to self-harm, a frantic attempt to replace the unmanageable emotional pain with a manageable physical one.

I was at first told that Ellen lacked the intelligence ever to learn any speech. So the day (at about the age of 7) when she shouted "Shut your face!" at her sister who was annoying her, I cried with joy because it was so completely appropriate in context. She clearly understood the situation and was able to articulate an apt response. She has developed a fascination for many things – music (her ability and understanding is amazing); mechanical things (especially hand dryers, the technical workings of which she can explain very clearly); transport, especially railways, and clocks which strike. These simple pleasures give her more joy than most of us get from a fortnight's holiday in the sun!

She has also developed a terrific sense of humour. I remember when the speech therapist decided to work on "why" and "because" questions. She handed a doll's vest to her assistant and asked, "Could you wear this?" "No," said the assistant. "Why?" asked the therapist. "Because it's too small," the assistant replied. They went all round the table with the doll's vest, asking each child the same question, and each child repeated the answer they'd heard. Until they reached Ellen. "Could you wear this, Ellen?" asked the therapist. "Yes," said Ellen with a cheeky grin, and put it on her head!

Perhaps at this point it's worth saying that I have no time for the kind of sentimental nonsense that says God needed a special person to raise a special child and that's why He chose me, etc., etc. I don't believe God is the author of disability, but I do believe He brings good out of everything, just as He did for Joseph in Egypt. So I would be lying if I said Ellen hadn't suffered a great deal. But the flip side of this is that when the smallest achievement costs an unbelievable effort, yet she determinedly persists until she has mastered whatever it is, she experiences an ecstasy of delight that most of us would envy. Her lows are lower, but her highs are higher, than most people's. Perhaps that's a way of saying that she lives more fully and is more truly human than the rest of us.

But once I have put these three arguments to the class I will explain that there are two still more powerful reasons why I believe that disability is no reason for abortion. Firstly, abortion is the ultimate form of disability discrimination. We now, quite rightly, have equality laws that preclude shops, educational establishments, places of entertainment or of worship, modes of transport, etc., from discriminating against anybody on the grounds of disability. So why is it considered acceptable to eliminate people before birth on the grounds of their disability? You do not have to be a person of faith to understand this. It's not a matter of religion, charity, or even simply of morality. It's a matter of justice. In any case, what would such a policy achieve? It's a fact that only about 17% of disabled people are born with their disabilities, so even if every single one of them had been aborted, 83% of disabled people would remain. Once we accept that the unborn are unacceptable as members of society if they don't conform to our ideal of physical or intellectual perfection, it's a chillingly small step towards the conclusion that burdensome disabled people ought to opt for euthanasia. I could at this point invoke examples of disabled high-achievers such as Dame Tanni Grey-Thompson, Professor Stephen Hawking or the amazingly talented musician, Stevie Wonder. But I won't. Because every disabled person, even those whose herculean efforts result in achievements that seem very small to us, is of infinite worth.

And that brings me to my most important point. The Bible affirms that we are of incalculable worth because we are made in God's own image. David expressed it in Psalm 139 by saying that we are "fearfully and wonderfully made". The Bible knows of no exceptions to this, and nor do I. Every single one of us is the dearly-beloved of our Father in heaven. And just as my daughter's disabilities haven't made me, as her mother, enjoy her company and conversation any less, or love her any less than her sisters, nor does He value those of us who are blessed with a full set of working limbs and an absence of invisible disabilities more than those whose limitations appear greater. In fact, when you read the beatitudes, Jesus placed those with the greatest apparent disadvantages in life in the place of most importance in the Kingdom of God.

So I hope that my lesson will give these young people a different perspective on a subject they may never have considered very deeply. And I hope that, should any of them ever find themselves facing the terrible choice of whether to abort a foetus which they have been told has some kind of disability, they will choose life, and all the hardship and joy, tears and fulness of raising the fearful and wonderful little person God has given them.

Of God and Gardening

Spring is on the way and I am starting to think about my garden again. This is still a steep learning curve. Until two years ago I had never gardened in my life, but suddenly I had a garden all of my own, and I wanted to make it both beautiful and productive.

The flowers I've grown have been lovely. The first year I planted some annuals – sweet peas, petunias and nicotiana – and some perennials – lilies, alstromeiria and polyanthus. Last year I grew snapdragons, which were colourful well into winter, and bright red salvias. Last autumn I planted violas and more polyanthus as well as some dianthus. They are coming on well, and I'm going to have a colourful display by the Spring.

I've had some spectacular successes – two summers and autumns in a row I've eaten home-grown runner beans three times a week. Last winter my onions (grown from seed) didn't do much but I had a constant supply of parsnips and Brussels sprouts. This winter my onions (grown from sets) have been abundant, and the parsnips just keep coming, bigger than any I've ever seen in the shops, but my cauliflowers didn't yield one edible plant. Encouraged by last year's success with carrots, I planted twice as many and am still harvesting them. My tomato plants last year were spectacular, with tens of pounds of fruit. The sweetcorn I planted did all right in the end, but I hadn't realised it was going to take eight weeks for the seeds to start germinating. This year I will sow them much earlier and expect to get a bigger crop. I'll forget the cauliflowers and go back to growing Brussels sprouts.

Some of my runner beans became too large and stringy to eat, so I saved them for seed. This week I found them in the cupboard, and they set me thinking. Come February I shall get out my polytunnels and start sowing. I shall look at those bean seeds – too many for the available space – and begin to select the ones I want to plant.

And that's what started me thinking. I'm not a determinist. I don't believe we're a collection of genes programmed to behave in ways beyond our conscious control. I'm not sure I'm totally an open theist either, although I'm part way there. Open theism suggests that the future is not predestined, or even foreknown by God, but that, since He gives us free will, He is open to us choosing any of a number of possibilities. A bit like me with my bean seeds. How well my beans crop next year will depend on which seeds I select. I'll make the best choice I can based on how healthy the seeds appear, but the final crop will be somewhat different from what it would have been if I'd selected different seeds.

Perhaps determinism, predestination and open theism all forget that God is not subject to linear time. Richard Dawkins asserts that God cannot be omnipotent, because if He already foreknows what will happen, then He can't change it. I think what all these theories forget is that God is eternal, and so is not trapped in linear time in the way that we are. He can both leave my choices totally open to my free will, and know what I will choose because even though to me that choice (and its consequences) remain in an unknown future, to God every moment of my life is eternally now.

So, just as with my runner beans, I can choose what I am going to sow. I can look at what grew in my past, good and bad, and select the seeds of my future. I can choose either to sow more of the same and allow my past to go on replicating itself in a kind of spiritual Groundhog Day where I can never escape the pain of my own bad choices and the trauma of what others have done to me. Or I can choose to select the good seeds – however small and insignificant they may seem by comparison, like a carrot seed compared to a runner bean seed – and propagate and nurture those things.

My future is not fixed and unalterable, neither by deterministic genes nor by a predestinationary God. God is not so threatened by my choices that He has to keep a tight rein of control on them. He promises to bless me with a future and a hope. I might sow a few bad seeds and take a few detours on the way there. But as soon as I decide to look at the blessings, rather than the traumas, in my past and sow from them into my future, I can map out for myself a future that radiates with promise and hope. It feels like a waste to throw some seeds into the bin. But if (like my cauliflowers) they hold disappointment and unfruitfulness, it's better to let them go and sow the things that will blossom and nourish me.

I have been betrayed, abused and let down. But I have also been blessed, nurtured and cherished. It's up to me which of those I want to replicate into my future. I am choosing to consign some seeds to the bin and sow those things which will reap a harvest that can nourish me and those around me. God isn't determining which I will do; He is leaving the future genuinely open to me, with real choices, not imaginary ones. It's true that I don't know what the future holds but I know the one who holds the future. But at the same time it's also true that the future will be what I make it, and that the abundance and variety of the fruit I harvest in my life will depend on the seeds I choose to sow today.

There's a word for it

At my church this year we're studying the Gospel of John. Taking a year over it means we have the opportunity to explore the book in some depth, and I am enjoying spending a couple of weeks over a chapter.

Matthew, Mark and Luke told the story of Jesus. They filled their Gospels with details of His circumstances, the stories He told and the miracles He performed. They presented Him and let the facts speak for themselves, so that people could draw their own conclusions about His divinity. Matthew, in his eagerness to present a clear picture of Jesus as the Messiah – The One who is promised – packs in as many stories as he can in as few words as possible, often giving only the sketchiest outline of an incident, or even perhaps conflating two episodes into one.

John, by contrast, is less interested in presenting a multitude of facts than in interpreting Jesus to us. He comments a good deal more on the narrative, and he offers us the sayings of Jesus at considerable length, especially in chapters 14 – 17. And in the opening of his Gospel, He is concerned to present God as the creator and Jesus as the re-creator.

John's Gospel begins, as we all know, with "In the beginning was the Word." I have been thinking about some of what John had in mind by calling Jesus "the Word". Just as "in the beginning" God spoke "let there be…" and the physical world was created, in the beginning of His new creation God spoke a Word which would recreate all that had been damaged in the Fall when humans rebelled against God.

Jesus, He tells us, is the Word who is from the beginning, the Word who is with God and indeed is God. Or in other words, Jesus represents what God most longs to say to us. And if we have ears to hear, each of us will hear that Word spoken to us. We will not all hear the same thing, for as at the Day of Pentecost, each of us hears the Word in his or her own language.

The prisoner hears, "free". Those imprisoned by circumstances or by the words and actions of others can still know the true freedom that Christ brings. The dead hears, "life". Whether the spiritually dead who receive life as they open their ears and hearts to

Jesus, or the literally dead who are promised resurrection bodies. The rejected person hears, "chosen". The despised person hears, "valued".

The blind person hears, "light". That might happen literally, like the man in John 9 who was blind from birth until Jesus gave him the gift of sight. Or it might happen, as it did for Fanny Crosby who never saw in this life, but could still pen the words, "Visions of rapture burst on my sight."

The deaf person hears, "song". Again, there are examples where that has happened very literally in response to God's healing touch; but other examples where a lack of physical hearing has led to a great sensitivity in hearing God. The child hears, "come". The hater hears, "forgiven". The troubled person hears, "peace". The fearful person hears, "hope". The broken-hearted person hears, "joy". The cynic hears, "truth". The betrayed person hears, "faithful". The person who believes herself ugly hears, "beautiful". The weak person hears, "strong". The poor person hears, "rich". The one who cannot walk hears, "leap, leap like a deer"! Some may do so here and now, like the man in Acts 3 who was healed and went walking, leaping and praising God. Others may not see that in this life. But, like the little girl who was repeatedly told to sit down, and eventually sat down grudgingly with the words "I'm sitting down on the outside, but I'm standing up on the inside!" many of my wheelchair-using friends have already heard a word from Jesus, an invitation to dance, and are dancing on the inside.

I would like to encourage you to take some time in stillness to read through the opening verses of John's Gospel and in the silence ask God what is His word to you right now. And remember that whatever He says to you, it doesn't come in the form of a disembodied word, but it is Jesus, who is the Word of God, who comes to you Himself.

I wrote this for Through the Roof (www.throughtheroof.org) and it is reproduced here by kind permission.

I know where I'm going…

John's narrative of the Easter story differs from that of the other three Gospel writers in that it is a much more intimate portrayal, seen less from the standpoint of an observer, and more through the eyes of Jesus himself. John, as Jesus' closest earthly friend, had ample opportunity to observe and listen to Jesus and to get a feel for how He Himself saw events. In particular, he records far more than the other writers of Jesus' own words in the period leading up to His arrest.

John records how, at the last supper, Jesus took a towel and performed the function usually reserved for the lowest servant in the house – washing the feet of everyone present at the meal. And he prefixes the story with this interesting observation: "Jesus knew that the Father had put all things under his power, and that he had come from God and was returning to God." The security that Jesus had in facing the cross came from knowing what authority He had, whose He was and where He was going.

John's Gospel makes three references to a character who is overlooked by Jesus' other biographers. His name is Nicodemus, and we first encounter him in chapter three. Nicodemus, a Pharisee and member of the Jewish ruling council, is fascinated by what he has heard of Jesus and wants to meet Him for himself. But, wary of being seen to associate with him, he cautiously visits him by night. "Rabbi," he says, "we know that you are a teacher who has come from God. For no one could perform the signs you are doing if God were not with him." – an admission which, at present, he lacks the courage to make in broad daylight or in earshot of the other Pharisees.

Jesus makes Nicodemus welcome, and has a serious conversation with him about the need to be born again, born of the Spirit, in order to be included in God's kingdom. He gently teases him in a way people only do with someone they like: "You are Israel's teacher, and do you not understand these things?" Nicodemus is forced to face the reality that, unlike Jesus, he does not yet know what authority he has, to whom he belongs, or where his destiny lies.

Nicodemus' encounter with Jesus has a lasting impact on him. He not only retains his confidence in Jesus' divine origin, but he begins to gain a boldness in defending Jesus to the religious leaders. When they denounce His teaching and berate the temple guards for not arresting Him in chapter 7 of John, Nicodemus risks (and receives) a rebuke by venturing to ask, ""Does our law condemn a man without first hearing him to find out what he has been doing?"

The final time we meet Nicodemus, he has flung caution to the winds. Jesus has been crucified, has died, and His body is about to be taken down from the cross for disposal. The normal fate of crucified remains is to be flung out into the valley of Hinnom, the place where the rubbish is burned. Nicodemus and Joseph of Arimathea boldly go to Pilate and demand the right to take care of Jesus' body. Permission is granted, and in broad daylight, in front of all the Jewish and Roman officials who have been present to witness the crucifixion, they tenderly remove the body of Jesus, wrap it in strips of linen and Nicodemus applies seventy-five pounds of spices which he has brought with him for the purpose. It has been estimated that such a quantity of spices would have cost the equivalent of about £110,000 in today's money.

Nicodemus is making a very bold and very public statement about his estimation of Jesus' worth. What a journey this man has come from the timidity that had him scurrying furtively to Jesus at night. Somewhere along the way he has learned what authority he has, whose he is, and where his final destiny lies. This has not come through any intellectual process of reasoning, but simply through keeping company with Jesus, feeling the warmth of His appreciation and acceptance, and realising his worth in God's eyes.

And what about us? We all arrive at adulthood hampered by things that make us insecure and uncertain of our identity, whether that is the result of a physical or learning disability we've grown up with, abuse or neglect in childhood, being the victim of school bullies, or even just the self-doubt and longing for acceptance that are part of the normal experience of adolescence.

From there we have a choice. We can either go through life hamstrung by these limitations that we or others have placed on us. Or, like Nicodemus, we can associate freely and regularly with Jesus, observing His confidence and security that come from knowing what the Father has given Him, His total acceptance and belonging to the Father, and His ultimate destiny in taking the full place the Father has reserved for Him.

So, this Easter, let's not continue to dwell on the things that hold us back or make us feel inadequate. Instead, let's be confident in our authority (for Jesus said, "All authority has been given to me... go in My name"), in whose we are (for Jesus said, "You did not choose Me but I chose you... I no longer call you servants... instead I have called you friends") and where we are going, that our destiny is inextricably bound up with that of Jesus (for Jesus said, "I go to prepare a place for you, that where I am you may be also"). Armed with these three confidences we can face with complete trust in God anything that lies ahead, knowing as Nicodemus eventually did, that our allegiance to Jesus matters more than anything, and is worth any sacrifice of reputation or wealth.

As C.T. Studd said, when he gave up a glittering international cricket career and an inherited fortune to take the Gospel to parts of the world where Jesus was unknown, "If Jesus Christ be God and died for me, then no sacrifice is too great for me to make for Him."

I wrote this for Through the Roof (www.throughtheroof.org) and it is reproduced here by kind permission.

Who are the disabled ones?

The day my second child was born, my world changed forever. She was thirteen weeks premature and the doctors had been warning me to expect her to be stillborn. Even if she was alive, they said, she wouldn't cry, as her lungs would be too immature. Moments after she was born I heard her give a fairly powerful cry – it was, and remains, the most wonderful sound I've ever heard in my life.

Now began her long, hard fight to hold on to life. It was more than ten weeks before the doctors could tell us that she would live, and at least two years before we could say with confidence that her life was no longer in danger.

From her birth onwards our world was turned upside down. I wrestled with God over what was happening, as I came to grips with a world of sleepless nights, emergency resuscitations, failure to thrive, physiotherapy and low, low educational expectations. Things that my other daughters received by right (such as appropriate education) had to be fought for tooth and nail.

Again and again Ellen defied the prognosis and achieved things we had been told were beyond her. For example, we were told she hadn't the intelligence to learn any speech and now at the age of 30 she can not only hold a conversation (on her own terms!) but has a reading age of 8. Nonetheless, her learning disabilities are considerable, and as a result much about the world remains puzzling, confusing and frightening to her.

One thing I observed as she grew up was the simplicity and yet the undoubted reality of her faith in God. Her music therapist at school (not as far as I know herself a committed Christian) remarked that Ellen was clearly developing her own faith and kept asking for songs about God's love during their music therapy sessions – so she was becoming, in her own way, an evangelist, too! By her late teens she was clearly expressing in simple words her own faith in Jesus. We asked her if she would like to be baptised and she replied with a very enthusiastic "Yes!" So we found a couple of strong friends to carry her from her wheelchair to the baptistry and she was baptised at the age of 19.

This caused me to reflect on my own relationship with God. How often I needed my questions answered before I felt safe to trust Him; how I needed to be able to work out logical reasons for my faith along with my experience of God; how important it was to me to be able to explain exactly why I believed what I did. None of that was needed for Ellen. She constantly flung herself into the arms of her heavenly Father, certain that He was there and would hold her. She saw things that I, with all my theological study, could not see because my spiritual eyes were dim.

In 1 Corinthians 1.20, 25 and 27 Paul writes, "Where is the wise person? Where is the teacher of the law? Where is the philosopher of this age? Has not God made foolish the wisdom of the world?.... For the foolishness of God is wiser than human wisdom, and the weakness of God is stronger than human strength.... But God chose the foolish things of the world to shame the wise; God chose the weak things of the world to shame the strong."

Amos Yong wrote these words: "If people with intellectual disabilities represent the foolishness of the world, what hinders our viewing them as embodying the wisdom of God?"

I suspect that when the world is wound up and all things are made new, and we begin to find out what things in our lives were of eternal value, and what things have passed away with the temporal world, we will have to revise our whole view of disability. We who thought we had the advantages in life – the strong, the clever, the ones the world regards as gifted – will find that on a spiritual level we have been severely disabled compared to our brothers and sisters who lacked those intellectual giftings, but whose spiritual life is marked by abilities and giftings we never knew they possessed. In that day they will be our teachers, leading us from the place of our spiritual impoverishment on the long road to catch up with where they already are in their deep understanding of, and relationship with, God.

I wrote this for Through the Roof (http://www.throughtheroof.org) and it is reproduced here by kind permission.

Adlestrop

Last Saturday I finally fulfilled a thirty five year ambition. Ever since, as a student, I discovered Edward Thomas's poem, "Adlestrop" I have wanted to visit the village of Adlestrop. His poem, about the time the express train made an unwonted stop there on a hot June day, brings it to life in such vivid detail, I longed to see if my imagined version of it bore a resemblance to the actual place. His poem describes the wild flower meadow and the haycocks visible from the station, but it focuses more on the sounds – the hiss of the steam, a cough, a blackbird breaking into song and being joined by "all the birds/ of Oxfordshire and Gloucestershire".

On Saturday I made my way from Hampshire to Birmingham ready for the Enabling Church conference and decided to take a detour through Oxfordshire to Gloucestershire and visit the place at last.

I pulled up in the village and parked in the car park by the village hall. A wooden shelter proclaims the name of the village, Adlestrop, in large letters, and on a bench under its roof is a plaque containing the full text of the poem. I saw the willows and willowherb though there were no haycocks to be seen. And yes, the air was still filled with that glorious birdsong, although it was a warm May afternoon, and not a hot June one. I didn't notice a lone blackbird, but I'm sure I heard pretty well all the birds of Oxfordshire and Gloucestershire. I had the time to wander slowly down the country lanes, taking it all in. I was happy when I arrived, but the peace and beauty of the place lifted my spirits still more, and I left in a state of elation.

And it suddenly struck me that there was a parallel with my life as a follower of Jesus. For many years, I read the book. I studied it. I became very familiar with its contents. I knew how they should be interpreted and was quick to argue with anyone who misinterpreted or misquoted it. But I never visited the place.

Proverbs 18.10 tells us that the name of the Lord is a strong tower. In the end it was trouble that drove me to the strong tower, and I began to discover the place for myself. I found that in Jesus there is such a place of safety, it can shield you no matter what life throws at you. The sound of His voice, which I had read of in His book, was suddenly real and present to me.

I learned not only to study the Bible (as good as that was) but to still and quiet my soul, and I discovered that in the silence and solitude, when I took the time to make myself present to God, He was always there.

Everything I had read and studied was true – but there was so much more which I had never imagined, depths of compassion, strength and patience which took my breath away.

Just as Adlestrop was so much more tranquil and lovely than I had pictured, so the place of safety when I pressed in close to Jesus was more wonderful than I had ever realised from reading other people's experience of Him. Just as I left Adlestrop in a more joyous mood than when I arrived, so those encounters with Jesus have changed me and left me happier and more at peace.

So I pray that whatever your circumstances right now, and however busy you are, you will manage to take time to find that place of encounter with Him and will find that everything you have read in His word is true, but there is so much more, and that your rendezvous with Him will leave a permanent mark on you of quiet contentment, and a thirst that keeps you coming back for more.

Adlestrop by Edward Thomas 1878 – 1917

Yes, I remember Adlestrop –
The name, because one afternoon
Of heat the express-train drew up there
Unwontedly. It was late June.

The steam hissed. Someone cleared his throat.
No one left and no one came
On the bare platform. What I saw
Was Adlestrop – only the name

And willows, willow-herb, and grass,
And meadowsweet, and haycocks dry,
No whit less still and lonely fair
Than the high cloudlets in the sky.

And for that minute a blackbird sang
Close by, and round him, mistier,

Farther and farther, all the birds
Of Oxfordshire and Gloucestershire.

I wrote and recorded this for Through the Roof's June 2014 Podcast
and it is reproduced here by kind permission.

Questions, questions....

Around 30 years ago I was just beginning to discover the extent of my daughter's disabilities. She had failed to meet any of the normal milestones during the first year of her life, was not moving around, sitting unsupported, picking up toys (or anything else), moving her head or forming any intelligible words, and already the tightness of her muscles was beginning to pull her little body into a distorted shape. A paediatrician came to visit us at home with the diagnosis; she told us that Ellen had cerebral palsy, with "spastic limbs" and might lack the intelligence ever to learn any speech (which turned out to be overly-pessimistic). After she had gone away, I put Ellen to bed and as I looked down at her twisted form on the mattress of the Moses basket which she was still tiny enough to fit into, a poem of sorts formed itself in my mind:

Limbs like a corpse, too stiff to play,
Voice that says nothing to no one all day;
No wonder, then, pillowed alone in the dark,
You coil yourself into a question mark.

Over the years that question mark came to symbolise so many things for me: Where was Ellen's guardian angel the day when her catastrophic breathing collapse caused major brain damage at the age of nine weeks? Surely this couldn't be God's will; but what kind of God permits things that are not His will? As part of my degree course I had studied several theodicies (ways in which Christian thinkers down the centuries have tried to reconcile evil and suffering with the existence of an all-powerful, all-knowing and all-loving God). I knew which ones I found convincing in theory, but in the face of the actual suffering, both physical and emotional, which I had to watch Ellen endure, all of them rang hollow.

And yet alongside the questions I was finding an ever-deepening embrace in the love of God. Somehow, as my experience of His love grew larger, the questions grew smaller. They don't go away – there are some I would still dearly love answers to. But first of all I came to see that the answers were not important as the questions; because asking the questions was an act of honesty with God, and being real with Him drew me ever closer towards Him. And secondly, in that growing closeness, I came to experience Him as utterly trustworthy. He holds my questions for me, and for now I am content to leave them there and know that whatever the answer is, it all has to do with Ellen's ultimate good and blessing.

As an A level student, I had read Camus' "La Peste" in which a Catholic priest watches a tiny child die in agony from the plague, and then asks, in his next Sunday sermon, "Who are we to say that even a whole eternity of bliss could possibly compensate for a single instant of human suffering?" As a degree student I remember writing an essay about the man born blind from John chapter 9, in which I explored the idea that to inflict him with blindness so that God could display His own works through him seems like the action of a megalomaniac. Now I came to understand that it was far better and more blessed for the man to have been born blind and to have been healed than if he had been born sighted in the first place. Somehow, every instant of Ellen's suffering was working for her an eternal weight of glory. And I believe I can say that without at all meaning that God caused, willed or planned her suffering.

When she was 4 years old we went to a large, international conference headed by a well-known evangelist (I am not going to name or criticise him; he is someone for whom I had, and retain, a great deal of respect). Among the congregation was a man who'd had a leg amputated. At the first appeal for healing prayer, he made his way to the front on his crutches, and asked for prayer that his leg would grow back. In this article I'm less concerned with that than with the attitude of the congregation. This man went forward with the same prayer request at every meeting. As the week went on, he didn't wait for the appeal, he simply went forward before the sermon ended. I began to hear people talking about him. I noticed that people would enter the auditorium and begin looking for him, pointing him out to one another when they spotted him. I heard people speculating about when he would go forward, whether he would wait for the appeal or go up during the sermon, and whether this spectacular miracle would take place or not.

During the conference another internationally well-known evangelist announced that he would be holding a healing meeting at 1pm. By 12.15 there was a 300 ft queue of physically able people outside the venue. Like other disabled people, our daughter could not queue outdoors for 45 minutes. When the doors finally opened, able people all rushed in to fill the front rows and get a good view. We, and many other disabled people, were relegated to standing room at the back.

The conference had been trumpeted as an occasion when great miracles would take place. It's not true to say that nothing happened that week. I personally witnessed one lady with MS who was apparently cured, enabled to get out of her wheelchair and walk normally for the first time in many years, and her joy was palpable – I was left in no doubt that God had given her a gift of physical wholeness and I rejoiced with her. But there seemed to be no understanding of the deeper healing that God can bring about even without a physical cure, and the results of the week certainly did not match the hype which preceded it.

During that week the impression I gained was that people had gone to watch physical cures as a spectator sport. There was something very disturbing about the way in which physically able Christians appeared to have come to be entertained by the misfortunes of people who had been promised a physical cure (even though God might not have seen that as their most pressing need at that time). I overheard people gossiping and speculating, and it was unedifying. As I reflected on the impressions of the week, I found myself turning to Mark 5, the story of the raising of Jairus' daughter from the dead. Verses 37 and 40 stood out to me: "And He allowed no one to accompany Him, except Peter and James, and John the brother of James." And "But putting them all out, He took along the child's father and mother and His own companions, and entered the room where the child was."

By contrast with the vast spectacle of a public gathering, when Jesus performed a truly outstanding miracle in which even death had to obey Him and yield the little girl back to her parents, He admitted only those people who loved her and those few who truly believed in His power. I thought of Galatians 5.6 where we are told that faith works by love. The kind of "faith" that manifested in that conference was not true mountain-moving faith because it was not fuelled by love. Perhaps there might even have been more physical cures in evidence if there had been more genuine love.

Over the years, I know that God has given me some specific promises for Ellen. I haven't seen all of them fulfilled yet, any more than I have had all of my questions answered. But I know that His love for her is unimaginably deep and constant, and my faith is fuelled by that love, as well as by my own love for Ellen. I hope that 26 years on from that conference, the church is beginning to understand that God's omnipotence does not equal doing things the way we tell Him to, and that if we do sense that He is asking us to trust Him for a miracle for someone, whether of the outward and visible or the inner and quiet variety, genuine love for the person is the vital ingredient to activate our faith.

I wrote this for Through the Roof (www.throughtheroof.org) and it is reproduced here by kind permission.

The Glory of Christ

Worldwide web watchers may have noticed recently that there has been some fresh controversy regarding a particular brand of prosperity Gospel" coming out of America. In this particular version, at least according to its critics, God has been portrayed as being rather like an over-indulgent grandparent whose offspring have only to name a wish for it to appear in front of them. If it fails to appear, there is something wrong with the way they are asking, the words they are using or their levels of faith. The focus of this type of spirituality appears to be our own happiness rather than God's glory. (I'm choosing my words carefully because the speaker in question claims to have been misunderstood and misrepresented; although the original words were, at least, ill-chosen.)

The problem with a version of the Gospel which emphasises God showering material blessings on us is not that there's no truth in it, but that it isn't half (or even one-tenth) of the story. I certainly know there have been occasions when God has blessed me materially. There have been times when praying for things has been answered by those things happening. There have been times when speaking out the truth of God's word has changed situations. There have also been times when I haven't received what I prayed for, for reasons known only to God, and other times when I haven't received what I prayed for, because I wasn't really asking in faith. I am also convinced that, for the most part, when God sees me happy, it gives Him pleasure. But these things form only a tiny part of my Christian experience.

Moreover, when God blesses us materially in these ways, we see it from our own perspective. We have a little need; we ask in faith; God meets our little need and sometimes even goes way beyond what we asked for. We are blessed, we feel really happy and we have a great testimony to share. But God sees it from a far larger perspective. He has only one real goal in everything that He does, which is, in Paul's words from Colossians, that in **everything** Christ might have the pre-eminence.

The times of most transforming, lasting joys in my life have come when God has not instantly gratified my desire, even for things that might seem a really legitimate good to pray for. I remember sitting in the paediatrician's office when my daughter Ellen was 11 and being told that her scoliosis was now so severe that it was crushing her heart, lungs and stomach and putting her at imminent risk of heart failure. She needed a very risky operation to straighten out her spine and insert a metal rod to support it. The paediatrician explained that the operation might kill her or leave her completely paralysed, but that without it she would certainly die. He concluded with the words, "We can't leave it a year. She hasn't got a year left."

For complicated reasons which I won't explain here, ten months went by before Ellen was able to have her operation, by which time her condition was critical. I was convinced that God can and does heal, and I could see no possible good to a child from having a painful and traumatic operation, so I confidently prayed for her healing. I confessed the word of God over her. The pastors from my church came round and prayed for her, and, in obedience to James 5. 14, anointed her with oil. (I remain convinced that they were right to do so.) I had every expectation that she would be healed. After all, James 5. 15 confidently asserts that "the prayer offered in faith will make the sick person well; the Lord will raise them up".

Eventually she went into hospital, but still my faith never wavered. I believed she would be healed at the last minute, the operation would not be needed, and God would be glorified by her testimony. When they came to take her down to the operating theatre, I was reading Psalm 27 aloud to her.

Ellen had her operation, and it was traumatic. But she didn't die and she wasn't completely paralysed, although she did lose some physical function. We were told that the operation would take at least 5 hours, she would need at least 48 hours in intensive care, and would be in hospital for at least a month. In fact the operation took less than 3 hours, she went straight back to the children's ward accompanied by intensive care nurses, and was well enough to be discharged 3 weeks later. I remained at her bedside day and night for 3 weeks, catching some sleep in a chair whenever she dozed. The thing that struck me was how much genuine, deep joy I experienced during those 3 weeks. I had an unassailable inner peace, and the presence of God in the ward was so real I almost expected to see Him with my eyes. My closeness to Him was deepened immeasurably, and the effects were lasting. It was an important stage in my spiritual development and, crucially, it revealed to me a glorious facet of the character of Jesus as the God of all comfort, which I would never have encountered if all my prayers had been instantly answered.

So to go back to the controversy about the "prosperity Gospel", when God blesses us with answered prayer it's not primarily for our own benefit (although of course we do benefit) but for His glory. And when He withholds answers to prayer, even to prayer offered in faith, it's primarily for His glory, although we do benefit too. Any Gospel which misses this point has an incomplete view of the glory of Christ – and this matters because it's the glory of Christ around which the whole of creation revolves, and towards which the close of the age will draw us.

In 1864 a puritan named John Owen wrote a little book entitled The Glory of Christ. If you can cope with 17th century language, or find a modern abridgement, I recommend it to you. In this book, he meditates upon different facets of Christ's glory – the glory of His love, the glory of His mystery, His glory as mediator, His glory in the church, and the glory of His eternal being. He shows how beholding the glory of Christ with the eyes of faith in this life is preparing us for, and will be completely overtaken by, our sight of His glory face to face in the next. Any Gospel which has anything other than the glory of Christ as its chief focus is at best lopsided and at worst misleading.

As C.S. Lewis discovered, when he pursued happiness it eluded him, but when he encountered God he received joy as a surprising by-product. Yes, our happiness gives God pleasure. But only when our happiness is derived from our pursuit of God and His glory. Any other kind of happiness brings him sorrow because He knows it is a deceit that will ultimately leave us empty and unfulfilled. He has created us for relationship with Him, and it's only in seeking to know and worship Him in all aspects of His character that we will find true and lasting goodness and joy.

This post was written for Through the Roof (www.throughtheroof.org) and is reproduced here by kind permission.

The thick darkness where God is

It's been a harrowing week for Ellen and those who love her. We finally finished sorting through her father's effects and, as she has asked me weekly since he died, I gave her his collection of cassettes and CDs. But music is Ellen's main way of communicating with, and understanding, the world. Every one of those music tracks reminds her of something about her father. She has been hit by a torrent of grief so overwhelming that her self-harming almost landed her in hospital and the doctor has had to prescribe tranquilizers. The bewilderment on her face betrays an emotion all the more crushing because she lacks the vocabulary to articulate it, and so cannot tame and constrain it in the way that words do.

I've spent today with her and, unable to restrain my own tears, I have found a curious relief in the discovery that my heart is not so calloused that it has become inured to her pain. I have had plenty of opportunity to reflect on the things God has promised me for her. It's almost thirty years since God spoke to me unmistakeably clearly about her physical healing, that it would be in the land of the living, not in the sweet by-and-by.

I spent my teenage years in a church that would have denied the possibility of God even speaking to me like that, and would have dismissed it as a misinterpretation. This tradition took a fatalistic approach to life which, while it acknowledged that God could in theory heal if He chose to, had no expectation at all that He ever would, and was more likely to view a sudden healing as a demonic counterfeit than a divine miracle.

As an adult I joined a church that took God's promises seriously and expected Him to live up to His word. I found this a much more satisfying approach because it lacked the gulf between faith and practice or belief and reality which I had been conscious of in my previous walk with God. (I still belong to this same church, thirty-five years later, a mark of the fact that the church has also not remained static but its corporate journey has mirrored my individual one.)

The problem is that neither of these ways of relating to God can confront and deal with the unanswered question, the question that would receive a glib answer from either of them: what happens when a promise remains unfulfilled for thirty years? The beliefs of my childhood would say that I was wrong to claim such a promise, and that is the end of the matter. I should resign myself to Ellen continuing to suffer as she does, and go on believing in God despite it all. The beliefs of my early adulthood would blame my inadequate faith or lack of prayer.

But both these answers are cop-outs. They are different ways of denying either God's desire or His ability to heal Ellen. What is more, both are counsels of despair. If God is powerless or unwilling to help Ellen, there is no hope of change. If it depends on my mustering more faith, I have already scraped the bottom of that barrel so often that I'm through to the bare ground.

It might seem that this leaves me no alternative but to doubt the goodness of God. Certainly that's a stage I have passed through (I remember once saying to my pastor that the Romans had it right, the gods are capricious), but I'm thankful that it never became my resting place. I am still expecting God to fulfil that promise; I do believe He spoke to me, and I don't believe the passage of time negates His word. But there is still no sign of the promise's imminent fulfilment.

I know this is a journey; who knows where I will be a month, or a year, or a decade from now? But here's where I am today as I witness Ellen submerged beneath a tsunami of sorrow, and desperately will her not to drown. There is a place in God where questions are unanswered. He is silent. The lack of any response from Him is the most deafening sound of all. And in that place is the immense relief of discovering that God is beyond my control. Nothing I do or fail to do can manipulate Him into acting in a particular way just because I want it. Which means that He is big enough to hold my most insistent, unanswered questions for me, and vast enough to sustain and embrace me in the middle of any storm.

A God whom I could command to do my bidding would be no God at all. Richard Dawkins has taught us to fear, or at least despise, the idea of mystery. But what would God be with no mystery? A God who was small enough to be comprehended within the little limits of my mind would be no God at all. I stand dumbfounded in the presence of an impenetrable and silent mystery. I feel I have an inkling of what Moses must have experienced when he encountered God in thick darkness.

It's like standing, some moonless night, on a deserted beach before an arch of rock, and stepping through the arch, expecting to find the cold sea lapping at one's feet, the wind chilling one's bones and the vast emptiness of a dark ocean stretching away for an infinite distance; but finding instead that one has stepped into a light, warm, soft-lined and homely room where the richest fragrance and the sweetest music permeate the air. Sometimes it's in the bleakest of silences that God is found.

Advent reflections

The approach to Christmas in our family is, as in so many other families, a time of growing excitement. Each day that the Advent book is opened, each chocolate from the Advent calendar, marks off another step nearer to the big day.

Ellen loves everything about Christmas – the lights, the shopping, the carols (especially the carols), the presents. That's to say, she loves the still-wrapped presents. She loves to take hold of them, clutch them in a moment of anticipation and then with her faltering fingers, slowly pull off the wrapping paper, by herself if she can, but sometimes defeated by the task and appealing for our help.

What happens next depends entirely on the contents of the parcel. If it contains something safe (i.e. familiar) all is well. If it contains something scary (i.e. unfamiliar) it is usually hurled across the room with a fearful cry of, "Take it back to the shop!" I'm sure it's a scene repeated in many homes where there is a family member with autism.

Over the years we have learned how to make Ellen's presents "safe". It's safe to give her CDs or DVDs as long as it's music and films she's already familiar with (asked what she wants for Christmas she will usually name a CD she already owns). It's safe, and indeed very welcome, if the parcel contains chocolate, bubble bath, money, colouring books and pens, a personal stereo or dictating machine or a roll of bubble wrap that she can cut into strips and take to church on Sundays to sit and pop during the long sermon.

Stray outside these boundaries and the gift will cause stress, fear and antipathy – very embarrassing if the dear old aunt who chose it is present at the opening. The reaction can be quite extreme – given the extent of Ellen's quadriplegic cerebral palsy, it always amazes me how she manages a bouncer that would be the envy of many an England bowler. This gesture can be accompanied not only by demands for the offending object to be taken back to the shop, but by mounting cries, screams and self-harm unless a swift promise is made to return the gift at the earliest opportunity.

Once again, as I make my preparations for Christmas, I can see a parable in Ellen's behaviour. How often do we ask God for something, anticipating joyfully the answer to our prayer because we know how faithfully He has answered us before; but then if the answer comes in a guise we were not expecting, we reject it and refuse to allow Him to lead us into a new experience?

I am lonely and want a friend – but I'm not willing to befriend the particular person God brings across my path. I want a fresh outpouring of the Holy Spirit in my church – but if it manifests in a way that is quieter, or noisier, or in some way more unusual than my previous experience, I'm quick to join those who denounce it as not being genuinely from God. I need financial provision – but God's response is to tell me to sow what I have in order to reap the harvest He has for me, and my fist tightens around the little I have, unwilling to make the faith experiment.

May God give us the grace to receive all His gifts, even the unexpected ones, and to allow Him to lead us in unfamiliar paths, in undreamt-of ways, into greater blessings than we could ever have imagined if left to our own devices.

Are you excited?

Over Christmas I have been reading and thinking about the ministry of John the Baptist, the forerunner of Jesus the Messiah. As often with the Gospel narratives, we have to fit the whole jigsaw together from the four different Gospels. Sometimes these Bible passages are so familiar that we have to picture them as though we were there in order to catch the real spirit and flavour of what happened.

John the Baptist as portrayed in the Gospels has a holy boldness that renders him fearless. He has a message which he will deliver to whoever will listen, and will baptise those who are willing to repent and amend their lives in line with his teaching. He even dares to call the religious and legal leaders of his day, "a brood of vipers". Affronted, they send a delegation to investigate the fiery young preacher. I can picture the priests and Levites coming to ask John just exactly who he thinks he is, and, as the conversation progresses, his growing alarm at the thought that some may be mistaking him for the long-promised Messiah (much as Paul and Barnabas must have felt at Lystra when they were mistaken for gods).

John first explains to them who he is not, and then goes on to define himself in Isaiah's words as the voice crying in the wilderness, "Prepare the way of the Lord!" So why, then, they want to know, is John baptising, if he is not the Messiah? I can imagine his face radiant and his voice fired up with excitement as he tells them of the One he knows is coming, even though he doesn't yet know who He is: "I baptise with water, but among you stands one you do not know. He is the one who comes after me, the straps of whose sandals I am not worthy to untie."

I see him on tiptoe, a-quiver with excitement, his eyes aglow, trying to convey to his hearers the momentousness of what God is about to do. And all this is a matter of faith, because he still has no idea who the coming one is, he just has one clue that the Holy Spirit has given him: "The man on whom you see the Spirit come down and remain is the one who will baptise with the Holy Spirit." He doesn't know exactly how this will look, but he knows for certain that he will recognise the moment when it comes.

And then comes a day when John looks up and sees his cousin, Jesus, coming to be baptised. John is troubled. He's known

Jesus all his life, and for a start, he can't think of one single thing Jesus might have to repent of. But more than that, he has a sense of being in the presence of one far greater, more righteous than himself, and he looks at his cousin with a combination of curiosity and unease as he blurts out, "I need to be baptised by You, and do You come to me?" Questions fill his head, as he looks at his familiar cousin through new eyes. Things he has been told of Jesus' history begin to fall into place. Jesus assures him, "Let it be so now; it is proper for us to do this to fulfil all righteousness."

And so, filled with a sense of anticipation, yet not knowing exactly why, John steps down into the river Jordan and baptises his cousin. And suddenly, the sign he has been told to look out for manifests right in front of him: the Holy Spirit, in the form of a dove, descends on Jesus as He stands dripping on the river bank. And to remove any doubt that this is the One whose coming he has been sent to foretell, a voice resounds out of the heavens: "This is My Son, whom I love; with Him I am well pleased."

And at once John understands his own reluctance to baptise Jesus. All the excitement he has felt as he has been describing the one who will baptise with the Holy Spirit and with fire now finds its realisation in the person who stands in front of him. His whole life has been building up to this moment; his faith in God has not been in vain.

Jesus goes on His way, leaving John changed forever; he has seen the Messiah, the long-awaited promise of God. The next day, as Jesus walks down towards the Jordan at Bethany, John cannot contain himself. He points to Him. "Look!" he calls to the crowd. "The Lamb of God who takes away the sin of the world." And maybe a voice from the crowd asks him how he knows, and still with that tone of wonder John replies, "'I saw the Spirit come down from heaven as a dove and remain on him. And I myself did not know Him, but the One who sent me to baptise with water told me, 'The man on whom you see the Spirit come down and remain is the One who will baptise with the Holy Spirit.' I have seen and I testify that this is God's Chosen One."

John's enthusiasm must have seemed fanatical and out of place to a society that had grown weary of waiting long centuries for God's promise. It was much more sensible to live a life of resignation than be at the mercy of hope. Hadn't many previous generations longed to see Messiah, and died with their hopes unfulfilled? Why set yourself up for disappointment? But John refused to be conditioned by the spirit of his community. God had ignited a flame of hope inside him, which he was going to nurture and not let anything extinguish it.

We, too, live in a world that is weary and has to a large extent given up hope of seeing God come in any significant way. More than that, many of the woes of the world, the wars that cause suffering, destruction and starvation, are caused by religious fanatics who think they are espousing God's cause. The rest of the world can be pardoned for thinking they would rather not be visited by such a God.

And yet we who know Jesus have a twin hope of His coming. We have an expectation of His ultimate return to bring justice and peace and to establish His reign and rule. And we have the hope of His promise never to leave us or forsake us. (Are we as excited about these as John was about His first coming?) Whatever circumstances we are currently facing, Jesus is certain to appear in the middle of it all! I remember being told by a preacher that an old Quaker Bible rendered James 5.8 "The coming of the Lord is at your elbow". Do we really believe He is that close?

I love J B Phillips translation of 1 John 3.2: "Here and now we are God's children. We don't know what we shall become in the future. We only know that, if reality were to break through, we should reflect his likeness, for we should see him as he really is!"

Suppose the reality of Christ were to break in on you right now? I would like to encourage you, whatever your personal circumstances, no matter what difficulties or struggles you may be facing, not to lose your excitement over the ways in which Jesus is going to come to you this year. You may not yet know how that will look, or what difference it will make, but like John, you can be sure you will recognise Him when He comes. Don't allow the general pessimism in the world around to rob you of that excitement. We have His word, the apostle Peter tells us, "made more sure, to which you do well to pay attention as to a lamp shining in a dark place".

No one in their right mind would turn their back on the beam from a lamp and step out into the darkness; and yet I know there have been times when I've done exactly that, focussing on the conditions around me rather than on the promise of God. But if you keep your focus on the promise of Christ, He will illuminate all your surroundings. So whether you are starting 2015 with a pleasant prospect of good things to come, or whether the outlook is grim, pay attention to the promise of His presence, His coming in your circumstances, just as you would pay attention to the beam from a lamp shining in a dark place. Soon enough you will discern His presence and see His transformation in your life.

This was written for Through the Roof (www.throughtheroof.org) and is reproduced here by kind permission

Thinning out seedlings

I hate thinning out seedlings, choosing which ones to sacrifice so that the others will thrive; but that was how I spent the afternoon yesterday. I transplanted as many as I could, in the hope that some would survive, but still, a large number had to end up on the compost heap. Even these ones, however, are not going to waste – they will help to fertilise next year's growth.

What surprised me (I was thinning out carrots and parsnips) was how much develops below ground before anything is even visible on the surface. Even some which had barely more than the tip of a green shoot showing through the soil had roots of more than an inch long; ones which were sporting two or three leaves had roots of two to three inches in length. I tried to select not the leafiest ones, but the ones with the most intact roots to transplant elsewhere in the vegetable plot, as I thought they would have the most chance of successfully establishing themselves.

It got me thinking. How often we look at the bits we can see in the soil of a life – our own or someone else's – and draw conclusions and judgements from that. I hear someone (myself or somebody else) say something unkind; I see them act in a way that is unwise; and I draw a conclusion about their spiritual state – they must be in a bad place spiritually or they would not appear so unChristlike.

Yet all I can see is some immature shoots poking through the soil, looking as though there is plenty of room for improvement. What I can't see is that in a secret place, away from view below the soil, an ever-deepening root is pushing down into the life source; and no matter how feeble the appearance above ground, maturity and fruitfulness are guaranteed, however long it takes, because something deep and strong is forming and becoming established.

That's why it's unwise to pass judgement on myself or anyone else; I can't see what God can see, I don't know what He knows. And it's also why God reminded Samuel that people look at the outward appearance but God sees the heart.

I'm not going to chide or nag my plants for not looking big enough or strong enough. I'm going to water them regularly, weed around them, and generally tend and nurture them. I guess that's what we should do when we see a fellow-Christian whose behaviour falls short of a standard we think they should attain. Not judge; not jump to conclusions about the parts of their spiritual and emotional development that we can't possibly know about; but encourage, nurture, remove the obstacles that might hinder their growth, and water with the encouragement of God's word – and then sit back and enjoy the beauty and nourishment that God brings from their life.

No Blame, No Shame

I walk this road quite simply because there is no alternative. I think, even now, if there was somewhere else to go I would take another route. But all other options have been exhausted. I try not to think of the distance because, weary and hungry as I am, I just can't contemplate the physical effort required to walk so far. And so I shield my eyes from the noonday glare and put what little energy I have into taking each next dusty step.

What a sight I must look, my hair matted with whatever dirt and undergrowth I've slept on for the past few weeks. I know I stink, and not just because I haven't been able to wash or bathe. The muck is clinging to my clothes and skin; some is even stuck in my hair. "How are the mighty fallen," I exclaim aloud. My voice startles the birds twittering in the long grass at the edge of the road, and they fall momentarily silent before resuming their chirping, unconcerned by my troubles.

Disgust and anger struggle within me – a tussle between shame and blame. I'm a disgrace. Everything that has happened to me, I have brought on myself. Or have I? What was my father thinking, when he agreed to my request? What kind of father fails to exercise proper control over his son? If he had said a simple no at the time, I would have had a tantrum and a sulk and then got over it. This is all his fault.

Or is it? Would I really have got over it so easily? Not with that self-satisfied prig of a brother breathing down my neck like a goody two-shoes. That was the real reason I had to leave. My brother was making my life intolerable. This is all his fault.

I'm sure all the neighbours have their own opinions about all this. I daresay I'm the black sheep of the family, not worthy to be part of their community any more. But what do they know? They have no idea what drove me to leave. They never saw the digs or heard the snide remarks muttered as we passed each other in the gate. It's all their fault, my father and my brother, this is all their fault.

Except it isn't. Whoever heard of a son demanding his share of the inheritance while his father's still alive? What was I thinking when I made the ultimatum? I might as well have told him I wish he was dead. And what do I have to show for it now? My father worked all his life for that money and I haven't invested it in one worthwhile thing. It's all gone and I haven't got so much as a pair of shoes on my feet. This is all my fault.

And so it goes on, step after shuffling step, blame and shame, blame and shame. More to the point, what on earth can I say that will prevent them from just driving me away? I bet they've gone round bad-mouthing me to all the neighbours.

No, that's not fair. I bet my brother has. But I've never heard my father say a bad word about anybody, not even people who cheated him or failed to repay what he lent them. Whatever he thinks of me, he will have kept it to himself. But I'm sure my brother will have spread enough ill will for both of them.

I have to think of a narrative that I can be saying to my father as I approach, before I get close enough for him to answer me back. Half of me wants to shout, "This is all your fault – you and that stuck up brother of mine!" But he's hardly likely to give me a hearing if I do.

Better switch from the blame narrative to the shame narrative. "Father, I have sinned against heaven and before you. I'm no longer worthy to be called your son." I'll only be echoing what he's thinking anyway, so I guess he won't argue with that.

What if he turns his back on me anyway? Better think of a follow-up remark so he doesn't just slam the door in my face. "Make me one of your hired servants." At least that way I'll have bread enough and to spare. And I can retreat into the servant's quarters every time the urge to slap my brother's smug face becomes irresistible.

And so it goes on, step after step, the thoughts swirling round and round in my head like the maelstrom at the foot of a waterfall. Somehow, step by step, step by step, blame and shame, blame and shame, the miles get swallowed up.

The fields along the side of the road just here belong to my father – I'm nearing home. I look up, in time to see one of our neighbours, a wealthy landowner, directing some hired workers in the field. He sees me, makes an exclamation of disgust, and turns his back. I'm confused. What is he doing in my father's field?

Gradually, the appalling reality dawns on me, and for once the shame reverberates in my head, completely drowning out all thoughts of blaming someone else. Evidently, my father has had to sell some of his land. Because of the share of the money that I took, some of our family's fields, the land that has been ours for generations, has had to be sold.

I slow my pace as I slouch up the road, not yet daring to look at the house I used to call home. Is there even any point going on? But where else can I go? There is nowhere.

Confused, uncertain, I hesitate, not daring to go on, not caring to go back. And then, suddenly, there he is in front of me. He throws himself at me and wraps his arms around me, pulling me close to his heart and holding on tightly. "My boy, my boy," he cries in a voice choking with emotion as he buries his face in my hair and the twigs and pig muck scrape against his cheek.

Without lessening his grip on me at all, he turns his head and calls over his shoulder, "Quick! Bring a robe and a ring! Get some shoes! Kill the fatted calf and prepare a feast! This son of mine" (and he squeezes me so hard I can barely breathe) "this son of mine was dead and is alive again, he was lost and is found."

I start to blurt out the words I've been rehearsing: "Father, I've sinned against heaven and before you. I'm no longer worthy to be called your son." But before I can go any further he places a hand on the back of my head and squashes my face into his shoulder, making further speech impossible. And hugged in that relentless grip, both the blame and the shame quietly pack their bags and slink away. Whose fault is it? Who cares? There's a love right here that erases it all and wipes the slate clean.

Who is the Greatest in the Kingdom of Heaven?

As you look back over our generation, whom would you list among the greatest Christians? Billy Graham? Matt Redman? Mother Teresa? Joni Eareckson Tada?

All these names are well-known, all are people who have dedicated their whole lives to the cause of Christ, and all have had an immense reach in terms of the numbers of lives they have touched with the love and grace of God.

But that's not how Jesus measured greatness. Here's what He had to say about it, when His disciples asked Him who is the greatest in the Kingdom of God: "Jesus called a little child to his side and set him on his feet in the middle of them all. 'Believe me,' he said, 'unless you change your whole outlook and become like little children you will never enter the kingdom of Heaven. It is the man who can be as humble as this little child who is greatest in the kingdom of Heaven.'" (Matthew 18. 2-4, JBP)

So, using Jesus' measure of greatness, who would you put in your list? Here are my top two.

The first is an aunt-in-law of mine. She died last year at the age of 99, having lived all her life in the house in which she was born. As a young woman, her father decided that she would not marry, but would be the one to look after her parents in their old age, and therefore she was not allowed to have boyfriends. She did indeed care for her parents to the end of their lives, while also working in a clerical job. By the time her mother died a few days short of her 106th birthday, she herself was 73, still rising early every morning to take her mother breakfast in bed. I never once heard her complain about her lot in life. Instead of living with regrets of what might have been, she lavished affection on her nieces and nephews and later on their children, and threw herself into the Girl Guide movement, keeping herself young by sharing fun, high-jinks and her quiet but vibrant Christian faith with generations of teenage girls. She was and is my heroine.

The second is someone whom I have never met and had never heard of until last month. George is someone whom our mission team met in Eldoret, Kenya in May. George's legs were amputated following an accident. He was fortunate enough to receive a wheelchair and so was able to continue working as a shoe seller. When he met a woman who had also had her legs amputated as a result of damage caused by diabetes, he considered her need greater than his own and gave away his wheelchair to her. From then on his journey to work consisted of dragging himself along the ground to the bus stop, crawling onto the bus which took him to work where he sat on the ground at his shoe stall, and then reversing the process in the evening. Our team was able to bless him with a new wheelchair and so his generosity to that lady was rewarded.

Both these people lived or live in a narrow circle of acquaintance. The world takes no notice of them and their sacrifice passes unobserved by most of the world. But God sees, and in His eyes they are among the greats, the giants of the kingdom of God. It's people like this who set the bar for us as Christians – may we imitate their way of life and grow in Christ-likeness because of their example.

(This piece was written for www.throughtheroof.org and is reproduced here by kind permission)

Beauty in decay

I have just come back from a week's holiday in the North Yorkshire Moors. The weather has been glorious and I've divided my time between reading and walking in the stunning North Yorkshire countryside. I haven't needed a coat – in fact, if it hadn't been for the varied hues of the trees I could have thought it was early summer, not October.

And this got me thinking. The trees can be truly spectacular at this time of year, especially in the golden autumn sunlight, but the reason for their beauty is that something is dying. The vibrant tapestry of colour is in truth a symptom of decay. And yet, within the manifestation of death is the secret of life, because these leaves as they fall to the ground and decompose, becoming subsumed into the soil, will provide the nourishment that ensures the ongoing life and health of the tree from which they fell.

How typical of God, to take something that is dying and clothe it in beauty! There is a parallel here to the way in which He works in our lives. This is true for everyone who follows Jesus, but perhaps it is more explicitly experienced and understood by those who live with physical weakness and disability, particularly those whose conditions are degenerative, for whom weakness is a progressive pathway.

Paul, with his painful eye condition, understood this well: "Therefore we do not lose heart, but though our outer man is decaying, yet our inner man is being renewed day by day. For momentary, light affliction is producing for us an eternal weight of glory far beyond all comparison, while we look not at the things which are seen, but at the things which are not seen; for the things which are seen are temporal, but the things which are not seen are eternal." (2 Corinthians 4. 16-18, NASB)

Like the tree divesting itself of its summer foliage, our bodies are in a gradual state of decay – this is the part we can see. But, just like the unseen microbes which bring about the eventual decomposition of the leaves, turning them into nourishment for the life of the tree, there is something going on in us unseen, something of the Spirit of God which is refining us and making our inner self more Christlike. It's not for nothing that the English word humility derives from the Latin word for the decayed, organic component of soil – humus.

If we allow the outward decay of our bodies to work in us the character of Christ, not only will the germ of eternal life be doing its work in the depths of who we are, but, like the autumn trees, we will find that there is something very beautiful about the process.

This was written for Through the Roof (www.throughtheroof.org) and is reproduced here by kind permission